The Forgotten Spark

2025

Table of Contents

Chapter 1: The Quiet Extinction of Wonder   1

Chapter 2: The Silent War on Wonder   5

Chapter 3: What Schools Forgot to Teach Us   10

Chapter 4: Why Adults Fear Their Own Ideas   15

Chapter 5: How We Learned to Hide the Spark   20

Chapter 6: The Inner Child Is Not Dead—Just Ignored   25

Chapter 7: Play Isn't a Waste of Time. It's a Rebellion   30

Chapter 8: Imagination Is Not Just for Artists   35

Chapter 9: Rediscovering Awe in a World That Moves Too Fast   38

Chapter 10: Why We Need to Create More Than We Consume   42

Chapter 11: Small Sparks — Daily Rituals to Reignite Your Mind   46

Chapter 12: The Courage to Make Without Meaning   49

Chapter 13: The Magic of Useless Ideas   53

Chapter 14: Trusting the Wild Direction   58

Chapter 15: Imagination as Self-Compassion   62

Chapter 16: When the Spark Begins to Return   66

Chapter 17: The Imagination in Others   70

Chapter 18: Imagination as a Way of Living   75

Chapter 19: The Return of the Spark   79

Chapter 20: Life After the Test Isn't a Test   84

Chapter 21: The Imagination Compass   89

Chapter 22: Fuel for the Long Road   94

Chapter 23: Five Sparks That Outlived the System   98

Epilogue: Light Carried Forward   104

Chapter 1: The Quiet Extinction of Wonder

There was a time when your mind moved freely.

Before expectations took root. Before judgment narrowed your world. Before grown-ups measured your worth in test scores and tidy answers.

You didn't try to be imaginative. You simply were.

A quiet room became a universe. A stick in the garden was a wand. A sword. A bridge to another world.

Imagination drifted beside you like breath. Wonder wasn't something you summoned. It was the atmosphere you lived in.

From the beginning, you were encouraged to believe in what wasn't there: Talking animals. Invisible friends. Magical lands tucked inside wardrobes. Wishes whispered into the night like spells.

Fantasy was your birthright. And for a while, everyone played along.

But not for long.

Because once you stepped into school, something shifted. Not out of cruelty—just design.

The systems around you were built for order. For answers. They weren't built to hold wonder.

The sky is blue. The grass is green. Two plus two is four.

This is how it is. This is how it works.

No one asked what you saw. They told you what to see.

You weren't invited to explore. You were expected to absorb. To remember. Repeat. Conform.

But here's the truth:

If you really look at the sky, you'll see lavender at dusk. Steel before a storm. Pink at dawn.

Grass? It glows differently depending on the light. Your mood. The moment.

Reality isn't fixed. It moves. It breathes. But you were taught to trade softness for certainty.

You learned to stay inside the lines. Sometimes literally.

You stopped asking strange questions. You began filtering your curiosity. You hesitated before sharing the stories you once told freely.

Slowly, the wild parts of your imagination—the ones that didn't fit inside a classroom—began to shrink.

No one said, "Stop imagining." But the signals were clear:

"Be serious." "Don't be silly." "That's not how the world works." "You need to focus."

So you focused. You adapted. You succeeded. You learned to meet expectations and get things done.

But something else happened, too. Quietly. Almost imperceptibly.

You began to silence the voice that once spoke in sparks. The one that made up songs. That danced without music. That built invisible worlds out of boredom.

Not because it was gone. But because the world had stopped listening.

This book is about that voice.

The one you buried beneath calendars and small talk. The one that flickers when you lose yourself in creative flow. When a song moves you for reasons you can't name.

It's the part of you that still feels something is missing—even if you don't have the words.

Imagination is not a luxury. It isn't an artistic quirk or a childish indulgence.

It's core. It's how we make sense of the world. How we innovate. Empathize. Expand what's possible.

Without it, we don't just lose wonder—we lose the ability to imagine who we might become.

If you've ever felt numb for no clear reason... If you've scrolled endlessly and still felt unsatisfied... If you've ever thought, "This can't be all there is"...

You're not alone.

That ache? That restlessness? That's a silenced imagination, knocking.

This isn't a book about becoming more imaginative. It's a book about remembering that you already are.

That part of you is still intact.

Maybe a little dusty. Maybe unsure of its welcome.

But alive. And waiting.

In the pages ahead, we'll explore what happens when imagination goes underground—and how to bring it back into the light.

You'll learn to recognize the quiet moments when wonder returns: A flash of an old idea in the shower. A childhood memory that tugs at your heart. A moment of beauty that doesn't need to be explained.

You'll discover how imagination is linked to healing. Not just expression, but restoration.

And you'll remember how to listen for the soft voice that never stopped speaking.

Because reclaiming imagination isn't an indulgence. It's an act of courage.

To imagine is to question what's been labeled as fixed. To wonder is to resist numbness. To create is to believe something new is still possible.

This isn't about escaping reality.

It's about expanding it.

The spark never left you. It's still burning— Quietly. Steadily. Beneath the layers of adulthood.

Let's go find it.

Key Takeaways

- Imagination is not a childish phase—it is central to perception, empathy, and possibility.

- Formal education often trades wonder for certainty and efficiency.

- Many of us carry a quiet ache from suppressing our innate creativity.

- That imaginative self is not gone—only waiting to be remembered.

- Reclaiming imagination is not indulgent. It's restorative. It's radical. It's vital.

Slow Spark Practice

Try This Today:

Find a quiet moment alone. Let your mind wander. No task. No judgment. No goal.

Just notice where your thoughts go. Even if nothing happens, stay curious.

That's how the spark begins to stir.

Prompt:

What's a strange or imaginative thought you used to have as a child—one that still lingers somewhere in you?

Write it down. Don't explain it. Just honor it.

Chapter 2: The Silent War on Wonder

There's a moment most people miss—when a child begins to hesitate before sharing an idea. It's subtle. A pause before raising a hand. A glance to see if anyone's laughing. A quiet edit before they speak.

You won't find it in psychology textbooks or school curricula. But it happens.

Not loudly.

Not through rejection.

But through small, almost invisible shifts.

It starts with a laugh that lands too sharply. A well-meant

correction. A sigh when a story goes on too long. At first, they still share. Still draw wild things. Still believe in invisible ones. But slowly, they begin to notice—how grown-ups wince or redirect, how other kids learn what's cool, what's correct. The world, it seems, prefers answers that fit.

In the beginning, imagination is celebrated. When a child says the sun is a dragon, we smile—not at them, but with them. When they draw a stairway to the moon, we hang it proudly. We marvel at their view.

In those early years, creativity feels like currency. It buys affection, praise, connection. We reward it with gold stars and bedtime stories. But then, slowly, the reward system changes.

The rules arrive. Not as punishment—but as preparation.

The sky is blue.
The grass is green.
This is the right answer.
This is how the day is divided.
This is what matters.

And some of it, of course, is necessary. We need shared structure to navigate life. But we often fail to see the cost: a quiet erosion. Not the destruction of wonder, but its burial under a new priority—compliance.

We start telling children what to see before they've had time to look. We give them facts before they've had a chance to feel. We favor speed over exploration, certainty over curiosity, replication over invention.

And so, the shift begins.

A child enters school full of questions. They wonder if trees can talk, if time can bend, if monsters might be misunderstood. But as they move through the grades, they start learning a different kind of lesson—one that's never written down.

They learn that the questions that count have answers at the back of the book. That neatness and precision matter more than imagination. That success means matching expectations—not exceeding them in unexpected ways.

They learn that imagination is not on the test.

And none of it comes from bad intent. It's done in the name of readiness—for exams, for jobs, for the "real world."

But we forget: imagination *is* the real world. It's the engine behind innovation, empathy, resilience, and hope.

When we mute a child's wonder, we don't just quiet their playfulness—we compromise their future ability to adapt, to invent, to overcome. The challenges they'll face won't come with answer keys. The solutions they'll need won't exist in manuals.

And now, the silent war on wonder has evolved.

It no longer hides in lesson plans or red ink. It's baked into the very tools we place in tiny hands.

We give children screens before they can even read. Glowing, moving, endlessly entertaining. Not designed to provoke thought—but to hold attention. Not to invite creativity—but to deliver content.

Swipe. Watch. Repeat.

They're good at it—so good we forget what's being lost.

Screens teach children to crave what others have. To compare before reflecting. To consume before imagining. Even the apps labeled "educational" often carry a deeper message: stay entertained. Stay passive. Don't make—just watch.

Even play has been repackaged. Branded. Instructed.

Once, LEGO bricks spilled freely onto the floor—open-ended and infinite. Now, they arrive as pre-built kits with manuals and marketing. "Build this ship. Follow these steps. Make it match the picture."

Creativity becomes assembly. Mistakes become frustration. Imagination is narrowed to a checklist.

And we ask: why don't kids invent anymore? Why don't they focus? Why aren't they more original?

But maybe that's not the right question.

Maybe we should ask: *What have we shown them?*

Because this war on wonder isn't just about kids.

It's about us.

We've stopped imagining too.

We move from task to task. We scroll until we're numb. We fill every pause with noise. We speak of presence while checking emails in line at the grocery store. We don't play. We don't drift. We optimize.

When was the last time you stared out a window—not toward productivity, but toward possibility?

When did you last make something for no reason at all?

We model a world that forgets imagination. So when a child hesitates before raising their hand, or edits their story into acceptability, we must ask:

Did they stop imagining?

Or did they learn it from us?

This war doesn't need soldiers. It wins through forgetting.

Forgetting to pause.
Forgetting to wonder.
Forgetting to protect the parts of ourselves that don't fit inside tidy boxes.

But here's the truth: you were born to wonder.

You were made to invent, to play, to imagine worlds not yet built. That part of you may be buried, but it's not gone. It's waiting—for permission, for quiet, for you.

This isn't a call to tear it all down.

It's a call to pause.
To notice.
To remember.

Because the moment you choose to imagine again—on purpose—you're not just healing yourself.

You're lighting a path.
For children.
For others.
For the future.

You're showing the world that it's still safe to wonder.

Key Takeaways

- Children begin censoring their creativity not through rejection, but through subtle signals of expectation.

- Education systems often reward compliance over curiosity.

- Modern tools encourage consumption over creation.

- Adults model behavior: when we stop imagining, children do too.

- Reclaiming imagination is quiet resistance—a return to what was never truly lost.

Slow Spark Practice

Try This Today:

Next time you're with a child—or your younger self in memory—notice your response to something odd or "wrong." Instead of correcting, ask: *Why?* or *Tell me more.* Respond with wonder, not instruction.

Prompt:

What's something you believed as a child that made no sense—but still felt true? Write it down. Now ask yourself: *What part of me still wants to believe it?*

Chapter 3: What Schools Forgot to Teach Us

You don't remember the exact moment it happened. None of us do.

It didn't come with a loud announcement or a dramatic loss. There was no final straw, no thief in the night. Instead, it arrived the way these things always do: quietly. Folded into an ordinary moment. A Tuesday, maybe. Or a Wednesday, when it was raining and the air smelled like wet paper and pencil shavings.

You were sitting at your desk. Tracing letters. Copying sums. Lost in thought. Maybe you'd just drawn something strange—a spaceship shaped like a pinecone, a bird with five wings and a secret message hidden in its feathers.

Or maybe you had an idea you couldn't explain yet, but it made perfect sense in your body. You shared it without hesitation—because back then, you didn't know how to hesitate. You trusted your mind. You trusted that what you saw was worth seeing.

And then something shifted.

It wasn't cruel. It wasn't even meant to wound. A teacher, maybe kind but hurried, glanced over and said, "That's not quite right." A friend giggled—not unkindly, but just enough to make you pause next time. Or maybe it was the red pen. The worksheet. The correct answer circled at the bottom. And in that moment, a quiet lesson was learned—one far deeper than arithmetic or grammar.

Learning, you were told, meant correction.
Not exploration.
Not wonder.
Not possibility.

This is how most of us were educated.

We were taught to look for *the* answer—not an answer, not your answer. The answer that matched the back of the book. We were shown how to follow steps, how to replicate what had already been done, how to recall what had already been proven. It didn't matter how we got there—as long as the result was correct.

Precision was rewarded. Curiosity, not so much.

Imagination became something peripheral. Something saved for recess, or maybe tucked into the corner of an art class that met once a week—wedged between math drills and reading comprehension. Even then, there were rubrics. Guidelines. Boxes to tick.

So we adapted.

We learned to raise our hands only when we were certain. To wait for permission. To silence the impulse to share something strange or incomplete. We became efficient. Accurate. On track. Safe.

And in doing so, we began to lose something we didn't yet know we were losing.

To be clear: this isn't an indictment of teachers. Many of them were lifelines—kind, generous, doing their best within a system that wasn't built for wonder. The issue was never one person. It was the structure itself: a system designed around standardization, outcomes, and order. A system that, in trying to prepare us for the future, forgot to nurture what could shape it.

Because what school rarely taught us—what was never on the test—was how to sit with uncertainty.

How to explore a question that didn't yet have an answer.

How to follow a thread of thought that felt important even if it didn't make sense.

How to trust an idea that no one else could see yet.

We weren't taught to trust our minds. We were taught to tame them.

And so we did.

We traded spontaneity for structure. Vision for validation. We started asking, "Is this right?" instead of "Is this true for me?" The part of us that painted clouds with secret stairways or whispered strange stories began to quiet—not out of shame, but out of survival.

Even the tools we used began to shift.

Toys that once sparked invention started arriving with

instruction manuals. LEGO bricks stopped coming as open-ended raw materials and began arriving as kits—with diagrams and a glossy photo of what success should look like. Just like in class, we stopped asking, *"What can I build?"* and started asking, *"Am I doing this right?"*

We replaced exploration with execution.

And yet, underneath all of it, something persisted. Something small but stubborn.

Because no matter how many facts we memorized...
No matter how many times we were told to focus, sit still, follow the steps...
A part of us kept wondering.

Maybe that's why, as adults, so many of us feel a quiet ache we can't quite name.

Why we scroll through our phones and feel nothing.
Why we stare out windows and long for something we've forgotten.

Where did the spark go?
When did I stop feeling connected to what made me feel alive?

It didn't happen all at once. It happened in hundreds of tiny moments.

Corrections. Instructions. Comparisons.
The long, slow fading of your natural sense of play.

But here's the truth:

That spark never left you. It wasn't erased. It was buried—beneath the layers of standardization and second-guessing. And if you want to find it again, you don't need a new curriculum.

You need a different kind of unlearning.

Unlearn the belief that there's always a right way.
Unlearn the idea that creativity is a luxury.
Unlearn the instinct to wait for permission before exploring what only you can see.

Because the real question—the one school never really asked—is this:

What does your mind see when no one else is looking?

That's where your aliveness lives.

Not in what you've been told to know.

But in what you've always known, quietly, all along.

You are not broken.
You are not unimaginative.
You are simply unpracticed.

And practice begins here.
With remembering.
With allowing.
With trusting that your mind is more than a tool for output.

It is a garden.
A mirror.
A spark that never stopped waiting for you to look its way.

Key Takeaways

- Most people lose touch with their imagination through small, repeated moments of correction—not dramatic ones.

- School systems often prize precision over originality, and certainty over exploration.

- We were rarely taught to trust ambiguous ideas or follow uncertain creative impulses.

- Imagination was never destroyed—it was sidelined. It still lives quietly beneath the surface.

- Reconnecting with imagination requires unlearning the quiet lessons of compliance and rediscovering the courage to follow wonder.

Slow Spark Practice

Try This Today:

Take a quiet moment to imagine something without any purpose. Not for work. Not for social media. Just for you. A strange animal. A city that floats. A weather system that sings. Whatever it is—write it down. Let it be weird. Let it be yours.

Prompt:

What's something school taught you not to trust about yourself—and how might you begin to trust it again?

Chapter 4: Why Adults Fear Their Own Ideas

For many of us, it begins as a hesitation.

Not a loud one. Not something we even notice at first. It slips in quietly, dressed as maturity. It lives in the pause before we speak. The slight shrinking of our shoulders. The sideways glance to check who might be listening. A fleeting flicker of doubt before we share something that feels too strange, too big, too *us*.

The idea itself might be vivid. Playful. Even beautiful. But offering it—letting it live outside our minds—suddenly feels risky. It feels exposed.

When we were children, we didn't have that filter. We shared ideas like we breathed—wild stories, inventions held together with tape, games where the rules changed midstream. We didn't ask if the idea was good. We didn't ask if it made sense. The point wasn't approval—the point was expression.

The idea came, and we followed. That was enough.

But slowly, something changed. Not all at once. In tiny moments that seemed harmless.

A kind teacher, rushed, saying "That's not quite right."
A parent, distracted, who laughed a little too hard at something we thought was special.
A friend who looked away—not unkindly, but just enough to make us second-guess ourselves.

And so, we built a quiet defense.

Not a wall. A filter. An instinct to edit. To protect our most personal thoughts from the sting of being misunderstood.

We learned there were right kinds of ideas—the sensible ones. The clever, practical, well-phrased ones. Ideas that made sense on the first try. We learned that novelty wasn't always welcome. That strangeness could bring silence. That being misunderstood sometimes stung more than being ignored.

So we adapted.

We stopped saying the weird thing.
We stopped writing the wild story.
We stopped painting, building, imagining—unless we already knew the outcome.

We got better at anticipating reactions. Better at stepping back from the edge. Better at keeping the strange, beautiful things safely inside, where no one could touch them.

By adulthood, the habit was so familiar we stopped noticing it.

We told ourselves we weren't creative.
That we didn't have time.
That life had become too full, too real, too serious.

But beneath all that, if we're honest, something else lingers.
Not a lack of imagination—a fear of what our imagination might reveal.

Because ideas don't just come from the brain. They come from the *self*.

They carry fingerprints. Longings. Pieces of memory. Unspoken hope. When you speak an idea aloud—especially one still soft and unformed—you're not just revealing a thought. You're revealing a part of yourself that dares to play. To reach. To wonder.

A part that might not make sense to others.
A part that might not be easy to defend.

And in a world that rarely rewards vulnerability, that kind of exposure can feel dangerous.

So we do the safer thing.

We dismiss the idea before anyone else can.
We call it silly.
We tell ourselves it wouldn't work.
We move on.

We scroll. We answer emails. We forget that we were ever on the edge of something real.

But the ideas don't stop coming.

They arrive in the quiet minutes. The margins.
While brushing your teeth.
Walking to the store.
Staring at the ceiling before sleep.

A phrase. An image. A memory that nudges you. A thought that doesn't belong—but won't leave.

They arrive unpolished. Imperfect.
They don't demand your attention—but they ask for your presence.

They ask, gently:
Will you make room for me again?

Reclaiming your imagination doesn't begin with brilliance.
It begins with something quieter.

It begins with *trust*.

The trust to let something unfinished exist.
To hold an idea before it makes sense.
To follow it just far enough to see where it might lead.

The courage isn't in having the idea. It's in *keeping it alive* long enough to listen to it.

You don't need to pitch it.
You don't need to explain it.
You only need to let it breathe.

Because ideas aren't distractions from life.
They *are* life.
They're whispers from the part of you that still knows how to play. The part that used to speak without filters. That didn't care if the story made sense. That just wanted to share.

The fear doesn't vanish overnight.

But neither does the spark.

It stays with you—in the quiet corners, waiting.

It doesn't care how long you've been away.
It only wants to know:
Will you come back without judgment?
Will you say: "I hear you. You're still welcome here."

And when that welcome is real—even the smallest idea begins to grow.

Key Takeaways

- Adults often fear their own ideas not because they're silly, but because they feel *personal* and *vulnerable*.

- The instinct to self-censor begins early, through subtle moments of misunderstanding or dismissal.

- We rarely outgrow imagination—we simply learn to protect it by hiding it.

- Reconnecting with creativity starts with trust—not performance.

- Welcoming an idea without judgment is a radical first act of self-acceptance.

Slow Spark Practice

Try This Today:

Write down one idea you've had recently—no matter how strange, incomplete, or impossible. Don't polish it. Don't explain it. Just let it exist. Then sit with it for five minutes. Not to evaluate—but to honor its presence.

Prompt:

What's an idea you've dismissed before it had a chance to grow?
Why did you let it go?
And what might happen if you invited it back?

Chapter 5: How We Learned to Hide the Spark

Most of us can't name the moment it happened.

That quiet turning point when we began to hide the most imaginative parts of ourselves.

And maybe that's the nature of hiding: It settles in before it's noticed. Becomes habit before it becomes memory.

It doesn't arrive with a crash. It arrives softly.

A pause. A glance. A slight turning away.

Maybe you were in a classroom. Full of excitement. Ready to share an idea.

Something wild. Bold. Delightfully strange. A story about a talking mountain. A drawing that didn't make sense—but felt true.

You offered it freely. Because the spark was alive. And when it's alive, we trust it.

And then, something responded.

Not cruelly. Not harshly. Just... enough.

A teacher, rushed but polite, said it wasn't quite right. A friend laughed—not to wound, just enough to make you shrink. A red pen. A quiet correction. A suggestion to stick to the brief.

You felt it. Even if you didn't know what it was.

A flicker of doubt. The sudden sense that your idea was less safe than you thought.

So you paused. Just a little longer next time.

Or maybe you didn't speak at all.

And slowly, you adapted.

We all did.

We learned to read the room. To sense when it was safe to be ourselves, and when it wasn't. We became fluent in self-editing. Masters of the inner red pen.

The wilder, stranger, more vulnerable parts? We kept them tucked away. Not because we stopped loving them. But because we weren't sure the world knew what to do with them.

So we adjusted.

We focused on what was rewarded: Clarity. Usefulness. Structure.

We became who we thought we were supposed to be: Capable. Sensible. Dependable.

We asked the right questions. Followed the right steps.

And for a while, it worked.

We were praised. Liked. Told we were smart. Thoughtful. Responsible.

We became experts in staying on track.

But underneath the approval, something else started to ache.

A quiet sorrow. The kind that doesn't shout—it lingers.

You feel it when inspiration sparks, but fizzles before it forms. You feel it staring at a blank page. Not because there's nothing inside— But because so much has been buried.

You feel it when a song moves something in you that you can't quite name. Or when you realize it's been years since you made something just for the joy of making it.

Still, the mind tries.

Even after all that silence. All that filtering. Imagination does not give up.

It sends offerings: Odd images. Strange connections. Flickers of thought that drift through your awareness.

They come in the margins: In the shower. In traffic. Right before sleep.

And for a moment, you remember.

You remember what it felt like to trust your mind.

But the habit returns quickly.

That instinct: Brush it away. Move on. Pretend it was nothing.

Because somewhere along the way, you learned a rule: Ideas only matter if they make sense. If they're useful. Polished. Explainable.

And if they're not? If they're strange or private or unfin-ished?

You hide them.

This isn't failure. It's protection.

A survival skill. Learned in a world that rewards certainty over curiosity. Conformity over wonder.

And yes, that protection may have served you once.

But the cost?

The cost is high.

You stop trusting your mind's originality. You stop seeing your inner life as something valuable. You begin to think of imagination as extra. Decorative. Unnecessary.

But the spark? Still there.

And reclaiming it doesn't require brilliance. It doesn't ask for a masterpiece.

It begins in the pause.

In the breath where you choose not to dismiss the idea. In the decision to let it stay a little longer. In the choice to let something exist—just because it wants to.

You don't have to prove it's good. You don't have to make it useful.

You only have to let it live.

Because every time you do, you remind yourself:

You are still someone who sees differently. You are still someone whose mind surprises itself.

And that's where it begins.

Not with applause. Not with certainty.

But with a quiet decision:

To stop apologizing for your imagination. To stop managing it. To stop pretending it doesn't matter.

You don't have to be ready.

You only have to be willing— To meet yourself again, right where your ideas begin.

At the edge of your thoughts. Where wonder has been waiting all along.

Key Takeaways

- Hiding the creative spark doesn't come from one moment—it begins through small, repeated reactions that teach us to be careful.

- Over time, we adapt by filtering our imagination to fit others' expectations.

- This self-censorship is a form of protection—but it distances us from our truest creative selves.

- Even after years of silence, imagination still speaks—in quiet, persistent ways.

- Reclaiming it starts with permission, not perfection. With letting something live, just because it came from you.

Slow Spark Practice

Try This Today:

When a strange idea passes through your mind today—don't rush past it. Write it down. Don't edit. Don't polish. Just let it be what it is.

Then sit with it for five minutes.

Let it stay.

Prompt:

What's a part of your imagination that you've learned to hide? Where did that hiding begin? And what would it take to bring that part of you back into the light?

Chapter 6: The Inner Child Is Not Dead—Just Ignored

We like to imagine we've outgrown the child we once were.

We talk about our younger selves with distance, as if they were someone else—naive, sweet, a little wild. We wear our seriousness like a badge. We fill our lives with structure and strategy. We tell ourselves that wonder, silliness, and curiosity were just part of childhood—something we outgrew on the way to becoming "real adults."

But that's not how it works.

The child you were doesn't vanish. They don't dissolve into memory or disappear into your adult form. They don't exit quietly, forever.

They wait.

Quietly. Faithfully.

They wait while you climb ladders. While you chase time-lines. While you edit yourself into someone understandable. Through calendars. Through commutes. Through meetings. Through milestones.

And then, sometimes—when the world quiets, or the light hits just right—they stir.

Not loudly.

Just a nudge. A flicker.

You feel it in unexpected joy. In unfiltered laughter. In the urge to sing in the car or dance in your kitchen. In the moment you follow a ridiculous idea just because it makes your chest feel warm.

You feel it when you linger longer than you "should," just because something about the moment feels good.

That flicker?

It isn't regression.

It's recognition.

It's the part of you that never stopped wanting to play.

Somewhere along the way, we were taught to treat the inner child like a weakness. An indulgence. We talk about them in the past tense, as if we've moved on.

But the truth is: that child—the one who lived without filters, who asked wild questions, who created without purpose—they're not less than you.

They might be the truest part of you.

They didn't care if their creation was useful.

They built sandcastles just to watch them fall.

Danced with no choreography.

Spoke without scripting.

Made a mess. Then made meaning out of it.

Over time, that part of you stepped back.

Not because it was wrong—but because the world rewarded caution.

You learned to be careful. To be serious. To be composed.

You learned to tuck away what felt frivolous. Not because it stopped mattering, but because the world didn't seem to know what to do with it.

But that child?

Still there.

They show up when a smell makes you feel six years old again. When a song pulls you into a memory. When you doodle without thinking. When you almost say something strange, and stop yourself just in time.

They've been trying to reach you.

Quietly.

And often, you've turned away—not out of cruelty, but out of habit. You told yourself it was silly. You didn't have time. That being "grown" meant being focused. Logical. Unshakable.

So you quieted the one who used to lead the way.

The one who once believed the sky could open into anything.

The one who found joy in a piece of string, a puddle, a half-formed thought.

Yes, the world asks us to grow up.

There are deadlines. Bills. Realities that demand attention.

But the danger isn't aging.

It's forgetting the part of you that still holds wonder.

Because wonder is not childish.

Joy is not immaturity.

Play is not a distraction from life—it's a doorway into it.

Reconnecting with your inner child doesn't mean pretending everything is easy.

It doesn't ask you to be naive.

It asks you to remember: You are still capable of seeing with eyes not yet dulled by expectation.

Sometimes that means painting for no one.

Dancing badly, and on purpose.

Laughing at your own joke.

Asking a question with no answer.

Talking to your plants like they understand.

Sometimes, it's simpler than that.

Sometimes, it's just asking:

"What would I have done when I was seven?"

And letting yourself do it.

Not to be cute.

Not to be ironic.

But to remember.

The child you were?

They never left.

They've just been waiting.

And when you say,

"You can come out now,"

they won't hesitate.

They'll come running.

Key Takeaways

- The inner child doesn't disappear—they go quiet when they no longer feel safe or welcome.

- Spontaneous joy, curiosity, and playfulness are signs your inner child is still reaching.

- Culture rewards seriousness, but the cost is often a disconnection from wonder.

- Reconnecting with your inner child is not regression—it's healing.

- Small acts of play done without judgment are powerful steps toward creative reconnection.

Slow Spark Practice

Try This Today:

Think of something you loved doing as a child. Making up creatures? Building with cardboard? Playing in the dirt? Narrating imaginary adventures?

Give yourself ten minutes to do a version of that today. No rules. No goals. No self-consciousness.

Let it be messy. Let it be fun.

Prompt:

What did your younger self do with total joy and no concern for outcome?

What would it feel like to try that again—not as nostalgia, but as healing?

Chapter 7: Play Isn't a Waste of Time. It's a Rebellion

There comes a moment—somewhere between childhood and adulthood—when play starts to feel like a luxury.

You don't notice it right away. There's no farewell party. No warning. It just begins to disappear, quietly, crowded out by other things. Responsibilities take over. Schedules fill. Deadlines tighten. And slowly, the things that once felt essential—games, pretend, silly voices, spontaneous dances—fade into the background.

One day you're building a fortress out of couch cushions. The next, you're checking your calendar to see if you have the energy to return a text.

Somewhere in between, the floor stops being lava and becomes something you vacuum on Sundays.

Imagination gets replaced with tasks. Play becomes a
guilty pleasure.

You start apologizing for anything that doesn't look productive.

People praise your focus. They nod when you say you're
busy. They admire your hustle. And because we want to
be seen as capable, we keep going. We grow up. We follow
the rules of time. We trade exploration for efficiency.

But the human spirit doesn't forget.

It remembers what it feels like to be absorbed in something for no reason but joy. It remembers the giddiness of
being silly. It remembers the particular magic of getting
lost in a moment—so lost you forget what time it is, or
what comes next.

Play doesn't disappear.
It just hides.
It gets pushed to the margins.

It shows up late at night when no one's watching. In the
car, when you're singing at full volume. In hobbies we
downplay. In conversations that spiral into unexpected
laughter. In weekend afternoons when we lose ourselves in
something that feels pointless—but right.

We're taught to see these moments as extra. As indulgent.
But they're not extra.
They're essential.

We didn't outgrow play. We just stopped being taught that
it matters.

We were told it didn't count. That it wasn't serious. That it had no place in a life aiming to be respected. Play became something for children, or vacations, or people with too much time on their hands.

But here's the truth most people realize only much later: The moments we remember most clearly—the ones that feel most *alive*—almost always look like play.

Dancing barefoot in the kitchen.
Singing with the windows down.
Wandering a bookstore without a list.
Making something messy just to see what happens.
Laughing until we can't breathe.

These aren't side notes.
They're the core of what it means to be awake in your own life.

Play is not immaturity. It's imagination in motion.
It's curiosity, given form.
It's joy that doesn't need an audience.

And more than that, play is one of the fastest ways back to your spark—because it bypasses judgment. It doesn't care if it makes sense. It doesn't require explanation. It just wants to be followed.

In a world built on productivity, play becomes radical.

To play is to reject the idea that your worth is tied to your output.
To play is to say, "I am not a machine."
It's to remember that joy matters even when it doesn't scale.
That spontaneity has value even if it doesn't produce results.

Making something just for fun is not a failure of seriousness.
It's a return to wholeness.

32

Play is a rebellion—not in the loud, defiant sense, but in the quiet way it reclaims space.
It refuses to apologize for its softness.
It dares to value delight in a world obsessed with control.
It turns ordinary moments into sacred ones.

You don't need a playground.
You don't need permission.
You don't need to be clever, or creative, or good at anything.

You only need to pause.

To give yourself ten minutes to do something that doesn't serve a purpose—but feels alive.
To paint without planning.
To walk without a destination.
To try something ridiculous, just to feel the strange joy of doing something ridiculous.

Play doesn't need to be earned.
It doesn't need to be justified.
It doesn't need to be saved for after the work is done.

Play *is* the work—at least, the work of staying whole.

In the end, we don't look back and remember the hours we spent being efficient.

We remember the moments we felt connected.
The times we felt free.
The days we laughed so hard we cried.
The hours we got lost in joy and forgot what we were trying to prove.

You don't need to be younger to feel that way again.

You just need to stop waiting for someone to tell you it's allowed.

Because it is.
Because it always was.
Because being fully alive is not a distraction.

It's the point.

Key Takeaways

Play doesn't vanish—it's gradually deprioritized in a world that worships productivity.

Our most meaningful moments are often playful, even if we don't name them that way.

Play isn't indulgence—it's a direct route to imagination, presence, and emotional renewal.

In a results-obsessed world, play becomes an act of quiet resistance.

Reintroducing play doesn't require big changes—just small moments of joy pursued without purpose or apology.

Slow Spark Practice

Try This Today:

Give yourself ten minutes to do something playful with no end goal. Doodle on a napkin. Invent a game while walking. Use a character voice while making dinner. Let it be small, strange, and joyful. Resist the urge to make it useful.

Prompt:

What did you used to do just for fun that you've stopped doing? What would it look like to bring a tiny piece of that into your day today—not as a break from life, but as a way to remember it?

Chapter 8: Imagination Is Not Just for Artists

Somewhere along the road to adulthood, imagination was quietly reassigned.

It became the property of artists—those with paintbrushes, stage lights, sketchbooks, and spiral-bound journals full of musings. It was boxed up and handed to the "creatives," as if they were its rightful owners. The rest of us—those who didn't draw well, sing in public, or fill notebooks with poetry—were gently encouraged to admire imagination from a distance.

We were told it was beautiful.
We were rarely told it was ours.

So we turned our attention to more sensible things.

We became grounded. Logical. Proud of our practicality. We followed paths that could be explained at family gatherings or job interviews. And somewhere along the way, the idea of using imagination in everyday life began to feel unnecessary. Not forbidden, but optional. A soft indulgence, not a serious strength.

But that was never true.

Imagination was never meant to be confined to canvases or stages. It's not a personality trait. It's not a hobby. It's not limited to those who can draw, or sing, or dance with grace.

Imagination is a human faculty.

A quiet, steady capacity that lives inside anyone who's ever pictured something that didn't yet exist. Anyone who's ever wondered how things might be different.

You'll find it in the mind of a scientist, adjusting the variables in a new experiment.
In the teacher who rewrites a lesson plan because the room needs something else.
In the doctor who spots a connection others missed.
In the engineer who redesigns a system—not because it's broken, but because it could be better.
In the parent, mid-bedtime meltdown, who invents a story that shifts the mood.

Imagination doesn't always look like art.
Sometimes it looks like resilience.
Sometimes it looks like flexibility.
Sometimes it looks like hope.

It's not about creating something beautiful.
It's about seeing something that hasn't yet taken shape—and reaching for it anyway.

Even in the most structured fields—law, finance, medicine, architecture—imagination is what allows people to move beyond what's been done before. The ones who make the most meaningful progress aren't always the ones who follow the formula perfectly. They're often the ones who can see beyond it.

Nikola Tesla once described building entire machines in his imagination. He could run them in motion, down to the smallest detail, before ever lifting a tool. His designs worked—because he trusted what lived in the space between logic and vision.

That's where imagination lives:
In the space between what is and what could be.

It stretches beyond what we've been taught to see and invites us to picture something else—something better, bolder, or entirely unfamiliar.

But here's what matters most:

How you see yourself shapes what you allow yourself to do.

If you don't believe you're imaginative, you may dismiss your best ideas before they've had time to breathe. You may underestimate the quiet connections your mind makes. You may ignore the flashes of insight that arrive when you're not trying.

You might assume creativity belongs to someone else—when in fact, it's been with you all along.

When you begin to see imagination not as a rare gift but a living capacity, something shifts.

You stop waiting for permission to be creative.
You stop apologizing for curiosity.
You start noticing how often your mind is already imagining—subtly, consistently—what doesn't yet exist.

Imagination doesn't have to be dramatic to be real.

It shows up in how you reframe a problem at work.
In how you tell a story to make someone laugh.
In how you decorate your home to feel more like you.
In how you prepare for change, or hope for better, or picture a new way forward when the current one feels impossible.

You don't need a paintbrush to be imaginative.

You only need to stop believing that creativity belongs to someone else—and start noticing the quiet, steady ways it's already working through you.

Because it is.

Because it always was.

Key Takeaways

Imagination isn't exclusive to artists—it's a universal human ability.

Creativity often looks like problem-solving, reframing, or innovation—not necessarily art.

Many people overlook their imagination because they don't see it reflected in traditional forms.

The belief that you are "not creative" can limit your ability to notice and nurture original thinking.

Reframing imagination as a capacity rather than a category gives you permission to use it freely and often.

Slow Spark Practice

Try This Today:

Think of a moment in the past week where you solved a problem, made something easier, or improved a situation without following the standard path.
Write it down—not as a task, but as recognition.
That was imagination.

Prompt:

Where in your life have you assumed imagination had no place?
What might change if you invited it in—not to entertain,

but to explore?

Chapter 9: Rediscovering Awe in a World That Moves Too Fast

There was a time when the sky wasn't just background. It was a living story, unfolding above you in shapes and symbols. You looked up and saw not just clouds, but kingdoms. Creatures drifting. Castles forming and disappearing. You didn't ask what the weather would be. You asked what it could become.

You had time for wonder then. Or rather, you hadn't yet been taught to move so quickly past it.

Because that's what happens—not all at once, but gradually. We begin to trade the slow, curious gaze of childhood for the focused, forward-driven eyes of adulthood. We learn to scan instead of see. To respond instead of reflect. We learn that stillness looks like laziness, and that wonder—unless it leads to something useful—is a distraction at best.

We don't mean to lose awe. We just start living in ways that leave no room for it.

The days become tasks. The hours become checklists. We train ourselves to measure attention by its output, not its openness. We scroll through beauty. We glance past mystery. We half-hear laughter. Even our moments of pause are scheduled, prepackaged, framed by reminders and notifications and the quiet pressure to make every second productive.

But awe doesn't work like that.

It doesn't show up on command.
It doesn't reward efficiency.
It doesn't respond to urgency.
It waits—for space.

And in a world that spins so quickly, space can feel like a luxury we can't afford. But what if it isn't a luxury? What if it's a kind of remembering?

Because awe isn't something we need to manufacture. It's something we return to when we finally stop long enough to notice what's always been here. Not just the vastness of a night sky or the curve of a distant mountain—but the way sunlight rests on a stranger's shoulder. The way music finds a crack in your armor. The way your breath softens when you realize, for just a moment, you don't need to be anywhere else.

Sometimes, awe lives outside you—in color, in sound, in shape. But sometimes it rises from within: in the quiet astonishment that you've made it this far. That you've survived things you never thought you would. That your heart still opens, still feels, still hopes—despite everything.

Awe lives in the in-between. In the unguarded. In the ordinary moments we've forgotten how to see as sacred.

It doesn't ask you to solve anything. It doesn't even ask you to understand. It only asks that you stay. That you witness. That you let something larger than yourself move through you—not as fear, but as grace.

And this matters more than we realize. Because awe and imagination are not separate things. One gives birth to the other. When you're in awe, you're not strategizing. You're not filtering. You're not editing yourself to match the moment. You're simply receiving it—and in that receiving, something inside you stretches open again.

That's where imagination waits. Not behind ambition, but behind awareness.

When you let yourself be moved by something you can't explain, you create the conditions for imagination to return—not as an effort, but as a visitor. It comes when you're quiet enough to hear it again. It comes when the speed of the world softens just enough to let the sky look like a story again.

This isn't about escaping responsibility or abandoning direction. It's about remembering that you were never meant to live entirely inside the lines. That part of your mind still longs to be astonished—not because astonishment is efficient, but because it's human. And deeply necessary.

So maybe the invitation isn't to try harder.

Maybe it's to slow down. To soften. To stand at the edge of your own momentum and ask:

What have I been too busy to feel?

Because in that pause—in that long, gentle breath—you might rediscover not just the awe you've been missing, but the part of yourself that still knows how to meet the world with wonder.

And maybe—if you pause long enough, and look up again—you'll find the sky hasn't changed at all. It's still telling stories. Still waiting to be seen.

Key Takeaways

- Awe is not a luxury—it is a natural state we lose when we move too fast for too long.

- Rediscovering awe isn't about grand experiences, but about allowing small, quiet moments to move us.

- Our modern pace discourages presence, yet awe and imagination both rely on it.

- Awe and imagination are deeply linked; when you open yourself to one, you invite the other.

- You don't need to chase inspiration—often, it's waiting for you to slow down enough to be caught.

Slow Spark Practice

Try This Today:
Step outside for five minutes without your phone. Look around without rushing, without labeling. Let your gaze rest on something—anything—and stay with it longer than feels necessary. Notice what shifts in you.

Prompt:
When was the last time you felt awe that had nothing to do with productivity? What did it feel like in your body? What if that feeling was a form of remembering?

Chapter 10: Why We Need to Create More Than We Consume

We live in an age of astonishing access.

The world streams into our hands. Into our pockets. Into our moments of boredom, of pause, of quiet.

At any time of day, we can watch someone build a house. Break a record. Cook a perfect meal. Cry into a camera. Sing into the void.

We see more stories before lunch than our grandparents saw in a season.

And in many ways, it's miraculous. So much to see. So much to learn. So much to feel.

But there's a quiet cost.

Not one we talk about often. Not one that feels like harm.

Not at first.

But over time, we feel it: The weight of what we take in

without ever letting anything out.

Not physical weight. Mental congestion. Emotional heaviness. The bloat of too many voices, too few releases.

We become full—but not with our own thoughts.

We're full of other people's brilliance. Other people's beauty. Other people's perfectly edited, perfectly timed expressions of life.

And in that overflow, we forget: We weren't meant to just receive the world. We were meant to respond to it.

We scroll not just for entertainment. But for a spark. We chase other people's fire, hoping some of it will leap onto us.

But here's the hard truth: Inspiration without creation doesn't spark. It simmers. Then it stalls. Then it sours.

Into guilt. Into numbness. Into a quiet ache that asks: "Where did my voice go?"

Because when we only consume, we forget that we can create at all.

We forget that we're not just here to watch the world. We're here to shape it.

Even in small, quiet, private ways.

Creation doesn't need to be impressive. It doesn't need to be clever or polished or good enough to share.

It only needs to be yours.

Write a sentence no one else will read. Draw something pointless. Rearrange the objects on your desk until they feel like a poem. Hum a sound that means nothing and everything.

Stitch a scrap of beauty into your day. Not because the world asked for it. But because it wanted to be made.

That isn't indulgence. It's remembering.

You don't need a platform. You need a moment.

A moment to hear your own thoughts again— Not the curated ones. The wild ones. The ones that surprise even you.

Because creation isn't about proving. It's about returning.

To the part of yourself that exists beneath reaction. The part that longs to respond. To speak. To shape. To wonder aloud.

And when you do? Even just a little? Something shifts.

Not out there. In here.

A pressure releases. A clarity returns.

And for a moment, you remember: Not what you saw today. But what you made.

In a world built on endless consumption, choosing to create is a quiet rebellion.

A return to balance. A re-opening of breath.

A reminder that you still have something to offer.

Not when you're more ready. Or more talented. Or more inspired.

But now. Exactly as you are.

So make something today. Not for likes. Not for legacy.

But for the part of you that's been waiting to speak.

It doesn't have to be brilliant. It only has to be yours.

Key Takeaways

- We live in a world overflowing with input, but imagination thrives in output.

- Inspiration without expression often becomes guilt, doubt, or paralysis.

- You don't need to be an expert to create—only honest, present, and willing.

- Small acts of creation reconnect you to your voice and agency.

- Making something, even imperfectly, is an act of self-trust and aliveness.

Slow Spark Practice

Try This Today:

Create something no one will see. A sentence. A doodle. A shape made out of scraps on your desk.

Let it exist without purpose. Let it remind you: your mind still makes things.

Prompt:

When was the last time you made something just for yourself? What stopped you?

What might happen if you did it anyway?

Chapter 11: Small Sparks — Daily Rituals to Reignite Your Mind

Refined Version

We often imagine creativity like lightning—sudden, electric, rare. A streak across the dark. A gift we don't control, arriving if we're lucky, or gifted, or in just the right mood.

And when it doesn't come—when we sit in stillness and feel only static—we tell ourselves the quiet story:
Maybe I'm just not that kind of person.

But imagination was never meant to be an accident.
It's not lightning.
It's more like a shy animal, lingering at the edge of the clearing. Watching. Waiting.
It doesn't respond to pressure.
It responds to presence.

And this is where *ritual* comes in.

Not grand gestures. Not rigid routines. Just small, repeatable acts that say:
You are welcome here. I've made space for you.

These daily invitations don't demand anything.
They don't summon inspiration like magic.
They simply open the door.

You might light a candle before you write.
Take five quiet breaths before the day begins.
Keep a notebook—not for goals or lists or clarity, but for nonsense and dreams and questions with no answers.

You could begin each morning by asking something odd:

What shape is my thinking today?

What color is this hour?

If my mind had weather, what would it feel like?

The answers don't matter.
The asking is the point.
It's not about logic. It's about attention.
It's about remembering.

Maybe you walk the same street every day, but this time you look up.
Maybe you rearrange the objects on your desk until they tell a different story.
Maybe you hum a tune no one else will hear.
These aren't tasks. They're signals.
Soft and steady.

And over time, your mind begins to notice.
It starts to trust the pattern.
It starts to return—not with fireworks, but with flickers.
And that's what you're really building—not productivity, not output, but *trust*.

Because the part of you that once offered ideas freely—the part that brought you questions and shimmering fragments of thought—may have gone quiet, but it hasn't gone away.
It's still there. Waiting.
It just wants to know that if it speaks again, you'll be there to listen.
Without judgment.
Without rushing.
Without trying to make it useful too soon.

Daily rituals are a way of saying: *I haven't forgotten you.*

Even if nothing comes.
Even if you sit with silence or stare at the sky and feel only uncertainty.
That's still part of it.
That's still the work.

Not the kind that shows results,
but the kind that slowly, gently, reopens a long-closed
door.

You don't need fire.
You don't need brilliance.
You don't need a breakthrough.

You just need to leave a light on.

Because imagination doesn't need perfection.
It only needs a place.
And when you give it one—simple, steady, imperfect—it
will begin to return.
Quietly.
Curiously.
Gratefully.

And that, sometimes, is more than enough.

Key Takeaways

- Imagination responds best to *attention*, not pressure.

- Daily rituals gently reopen the space for creativity.

- Small, consistent signals rebuild trust with your inner
  imaginative self.

- The goal is not output, but presence—and a willingness
  to show up.

- You don't need to be inspired to begin. You only need
  to *make space*.

Slow Spark Practice

Try This Today:

Choose one small ritual to practice for the next five days. Light a candle before you write. Ask one strange question each morning. Notice one detail you've never seen on your daily walk. Keep it gentle. Keep it yours.

Prompt:

What quiet, daily act might feel like a welcome mat for your imagination?
How could you invite it in—without pressure, without expectation?

Chapter 12: The Courage to Make Without Meaning

There's a quiet pressure that sneaks into our creative lives.
Not the loud kind that shouts, *"You're not good enough."*
The subtler kind. The one that whispers, *"But what is this for?"*

And just like that, something once playful starts to shrink.
It feels uncertain. Measured. Nervous.

We don't always notice when it begins.
It often starts with a perfectly reasonable thought:
I wonder where this is going?
But behind that question is a shift—a new expectation.
Now the thing you were making—doodling, building, writing, imagining—has to *prove itself*.
It has to be *going somewhere*.

And if it isn't?

You stop.
Not because you've lost interest—
but because the moment has lost permission to exist.

Most of us weren't told directly that aimless creativity was a waste.
But we got the message anyway.
We saw the raised eyebrows.
The quiet dismissals.
The way *"What does it mean?"* sometimes felt less like a question and more like a verdict.
So we adapted.

We learned to prefer structure over surprise.
Purpose over play.
Predictability over wonder.

It's no surprise that by adulthood, many of us believe imagination only matters when it leads somewhere—
when it becomes something finished.
Something useful.
Something others can understand.

But that belief slowly shuts the door on the very energy we're hoping to find.

Because creativity isn't a factory.
It's not a productivity tool.
It's a relationship.

And like any relationship, it needs room.
Room to breathe.
To shift.
To be sometimes *ridiculous*.

The child you once were didn't need permission to create something that made no sense.
They didn't ask, *"What will this become?"*
They asked, *"What can I do with this crayon, this thought, this hour of sky-colored silence?"*

They followed the idea because it moved.
Not because it made sense.

That's the courage we're trying to remember—
not the courage to finish something brilliant,
but the quieter, more tender courage to begin something
uncertain.
To follow a spark without a map.
To let the *process* be the point.

There's deep value in making things that don't go anywhere.

Because when you do that—when you create for no reason
at all—you remind your imagination that it's still trusted.
Still welcome.
You say: *I don't need you to perform. I just want to see
what you have to say today.*

And in those aimless, open-hearted moments, something
shifts.
Not always visibly.
Not always immediately.
But something *loosens*.
The grip of expectation relaxes.
And for a moment, you remember that you're more than
what you produce.

That you still contain mystery.
That you can still surprise yourself.

It's not easy.
In a world obsessed with outcomes, it takes real bravery to
let something exist without needing to become something
else.

But that's where some of the most meaningful things begin—
in the spaces where nothing is demanded,
and everything is allowed.

So make something that doesn't make sense.
Draw a picture and don't name it.

Write a sentence and don't explain it.
Build a tiny world and keep it secret.
Sing a melody into the quiet just to feel what it does in your chest.

And when the voice arrives—the one that says, *"This is pointless,"*—smile gently.
That's just the old wiring.
You don't need to fight it.
You only need to keep going anyway.

Not because you owe the world something.
But because you're remembering how to *listen again*.

Key Takeaways

- The demand for meaning can quietly choke creativity before it begins.

- Creating without a goal reconnects us to instinct, curiosity, and inner play.

- Imagination thrives not under control, but under trust.

- The process is often more important than the result—it keeps us human.

- You don't need meaning to begin. Meaning often arrives *after* we stop demanding it.

Slow Spark Practice

Make Without a Map:

Pick a moment today to begin something small with no plan.
It doesn't matter what—only that you don't know where it's going.

Scribble shapes with your eyes closed.

Write three sentences that don't connect.

Mould something from scrap paper or clay or wire without naming it.

Speak a poem aloud that doesn't rhyme, doesn't scan, doesn't make sense—but feels *alive*.

Do it gently.
No pressure.
No goal.

When you're done, don't judge it.
Just notice how it *felt* to create something with no destination.

And if a flicker appears—
that soft sense of something waking up—
don't chase it.
Don't frame it.
Just sit with it.

Say *thank you.*

That's the beginning of trust.

That's the beginning of return.

Chapter 13: The Magic of Useless Ideas

Every so often, an idea arrives without warning.
It won't look important.
It won't have a name, or a plan, or a clear destination.
It drifts into your mind like a feather—light, aimless, uninvited.

You might be brushing your teeth.
Standing in a queue.
Reaching for a tin at the back of the cupboard.

And suddenly—there it is:
A peculiar thought.
A playful image.
A sentence that seems to belong to something else—some-
thing not yet formed.

Your first instinct?
Dismiss it.
It's random. It's silly. It's probably nothing.

You feel the pull to move on before the thought has a
chance to settle.
Not because it's wrong—just because it doesn't seem
to *serve a purpose*.

That's the quiet bias we've learned:
The belief that ideas must *justify themselves* to deserve
our attention.
They must be clear. Useful. Marketable. Serious.
The strange ones, the soft ones, the ones that come wearing masks—
we're taught to let those go.

But what if those are the ones that matter most?

What if imagination doesn't arrive in polished packages,
but in fragments?
What if "useless" ideas are simply early?
What if they aren't answers at all, but invitations?

We forget:
Most beginnings don't *look* like beginnings.
They look like nonsense.
A word that doesn't fit.
A shape without a name.
A question with no clear answer.

These scraps don't shout.
They don't explain themselves.
They come to *test the atmosphere*.

To see if you're still listening.

And more often than not—we're not.

We swipe them away like fluff on a sleeve.
We think, *I'll remember that later,* but don't.
We assume, *It didn't mean anything,* and miss the chance
to find out.

But imagination, like trust, is relational.
It notices when you turn away.

The truth is:
Many of your most meaningful ideas will first appear dis-
guised as unimportant ones.
They won't demand your time.
They won't announce their value.

They'll arrive as daydreams.
As jokes.
As flickers.

And if you're too quick to seek meaning, you'll miss the
magic they carry.

Because magic doesn't always roar.
Sometimes it hums.

Those odd little thoughts—the ones that make no sense—
they're not distractions.
They're *invitations*.
To play.
To explore.
To follow a path with no destination.

They are seeds, not blueprints.
They ask to be *held*, not solved.

And when you begin to hold them—gently, without interro-
gation—

you send a message back to your imagination:
You're still welcome here. Even when you make no sense.

That's when things begin to shift.

You start writing them down.
Not all of them. Just one or two.
You don't demand they become something.
You just give them space to stay.

Maybe you sketch that odd shape that keeps reappearing.
Maybe you write the one-line poem that arrived while rinsing dishes.
Maybe you name a made-up animal.
Maybe you don't name anything at all.

You begin leaving breadcrumbs for yourself—without knowing where they lead.

And slowly, something opens.

You start to trust the process again.
Not the kind of trust that says, *This will be brilliant,*
but the kind that says, *This is allowed.*

The kind that loosens your grip.
The kind that lets you sit beside your thoughts without managing them.

Because imagination isn't efficient.
It loops. It backtracks.
It meanders and forgets itself and starts again.

And often, the ideas that seem useless in the beginning reveal their value later—
when something inside you is ready to understand them.

We don't need to *earn* our curiosity.
We just need to stop asking every idea to explain itself before it's had time to arrive.

Some ideas may never "go" anywhere.
But the practice of welcoming them anyway—
that's where the real magic lives.

That's where you begin to feel alive again.
Not because you created something brilliant—
but because you remembered how to *listen*
to what wants to be imagined.

Key Takeaways

- Not all ideas arrive fully formed—many begin as fragments that only make sense later.

- The pressure for usefulness can silence the early signs
of creativity.

- "Useless" ideas are often beginnings in disguise. They
test your openness.

- Welcoming unstructured thoughts builds creative trust
and keeps imagination alive.

- You don't need to know where an idea is going for it to
be worth keeping.

Slow Spark Practice

Welcome One Useless Idea:

Today, notice one idea that doesn't make sense.
Don't judge it. Don't try to use it.
Just write it down—one line, one image, one scrap of
something half-there.

Fold it into a notebook.
Whisper it into your voice memo app.
Draw it and give it no name.

Give it a place to rest.

Let it stay without needing to prove itself.

Repeat this tomorrow.
And the next day.

Build a small folder for these strange sparks.
Every so often, open it—not to make something,
but to remind yourself:

- Imagination is still alive in you.

- Still offering.

- Still humming.

Even when it doesn't make sense *yet*.

Chapter 14: Trusting the Wild Direction

We like knowing where we're going.
We like outlines, milestones, finish lines—
the reassurance of a plan,
the comfort of clarity.

We're taught to move with intent,
to build toward something that can be measured,
explained,
admired.

If there's no clear outcome, we're told:
It might not be worth doing.

But imagination doesn't seem to care.

It moves like wind through tall grass—
sudden, playful, uncontained.
It starts in one direction, veers off in another,
disappears for days,

then returns disguised as something else entirely.

It interrupts you mid-task,
whispers while you're washing dishes,
tugs at your sleeve just when you think you're being "productive."
It offers no maps.
Makes no promises.
It doesn't care whether it makes sense to anyone but you.

You might follow it for a while and feel foolish.
You might try to shape it, and it slips through your fingers.
You might worry that you're wasting time.

But then—one day—something clicks.
The piece that made no sense finally finds its fit.
The half-formed story circles back with new breath.
The dots connect—not because you forced them,
but because you stayed open long enough for something
deeper to emerge.

This is the nature of imagination:
not control, but *conversation*.
Not a line—but a spiral.
A rhythm.
A dance.

And to trust that—to really trust it—requires a different
kind of courage.

Not the courage to be brilliant,
but the courage to *not know*.
To begin anyway.
To follow a thread without a destination.

You won't always feel confident.
You won't always be able to explain what you're doing.
But if something stirs—quietly, insistently—
that is reason enough to follow it.

Because this is where the richest creative lives are built:
not on certainty,
but on *presence*.

On the willingness to stay near what feels alive,
even when it looks strange,
even when no one else sees the shape of it yet.

There will be moments when you want to turn back.
To abandon the strange trail for safer ground.
To return to something sensible, presentable, easy to summarize.

But something in you will hesitate.
Because that safety comes at a cost.

The cost is *wonder*.
The cost is the thrill of not knowing—and discovering anyway.

The most meaningful ideas often live at the wild edges of
your mind—
the places untouched by logic or perfectionism.
When you keep showing up, even without a plan,
your imagination begins to trust you back.

It begins to bring you deeper things.
Not just ideas that might impress someone else—
but ideas that change *you*.

So let the road curve.
Let the shape shift.
Let the idea grow in ways you didn't expect.

Not every direction needs a name.
Not every spark needs a strategy.

Sometimes, the most important journeys are the ones
you didn't know you were on
until you looked back and realized

just how far you'd been carried.

Key Takeaways

* Imagination doesn't follow straight lines—it spirals, pauses, and transforms.

* The willingness to begin without clarity is a powerful creative choice.

* You don't need a plan—just presence, and the courage to follow what feels alive.

* The "wild direction" often leads to discoveries we couldn't have mapped in advance.

* Letting go of outcomes opens the door to real depth, surprise, and personal truth.

Slow Spark Practice

Follow the Thread:

Today, return to something unfinished.
A line you jotted down.
A half-baked idea.
A strange image that wouldn't leave you alone.

Don't try to fix it.
Don't try to explain it.
Just sit beside it for ten minutes.

Add one sentence.
Sketch a shape.
Whisper something it might want to become.

And then ask,
"What might this become, if I stop trying to make it behave?"

You don't need to arrive anywhere.
You only need to stay with it—
a little longer than you did last time.

Even one step is enough.

Even one flicker is a return.

Chapter 15: Imagination as Self-Compassion

When we speak of imagination, we often leap straight to creation.
To paintings, poems, inventions.
To visions of what might be built, solved, achieved.

It becomes something outward-facing—
a tool for doing, for producing, for dreaming forward.

But what if, before all that, imagination was something gentler?
What if it was also a way of caring for ourselves?

Because to meet yourself with tenderness—
to offer grace where you've only ever given pressure—
requires a special kind of vision.

The kind that sees not just what is,
but what might be.

To imagine yourself not as a problem to be solved,
but as a person in motion.
Still growing.
Still learning.
Still worthy—even in the middle.

That's not just kindness.
That's creative work.
And for many of us, it's the most radical kind.

We've been trained in evaluation.
In comparison.
In the quiet cruelty of self-improvement disguised as self-worth.

We know how to look for flaws.
We know how to measure what's missing.
But few of us were ever taught how to look inward with softness—
to sit beside the struggling version of ourselves and say:

"You're still allowed to be here."

To do that—to imagine that you deserve gentleness—
you have to reach past the voice that says you've failed.
You have to envision a new way of being with yourself.
One where the pace is slower.
The words are kinder.
The judgments are fewer.

That, too, is imagination.

Not the kind that builds castles—
but the kind that rebuilds trust.
The kind that softens the world inside your own chest.

Some days, that might look like rewriting your inner monologue.
Not with platitudes.
But with truth—spoken gently.

Instead of "I should've done more,"
you ask: "What did I need in that moment?"

Instead of "I'm always behind,"
you offer: "I'm still learning how to carry all this."

Instead of "Everyone else has it figured out,"
you remember: "Most people are just as uncertain. They're just quieter about it."

This isn't indulgence.
This is resilience.

Because when you speak to yourself with compassion,
you stop waiting for the world to grant you permission to
feel okay.
You begin to grant it yourself.

Imagination makes this possible.

It lets you see yourself differently.
Not as broken,
but as becoming.

Not as behind,
but as in motion.

Not as flawed,
but as fully human.

Imagination reminds you that you are not static.
That your lowest moment is not your final form.
That deep beneath the noise of self-doubt,
there is still a voice waiting to be heard—
one that says:

"You don't need to be fixed. You just need to be met."

And when you begin to meet yourself with wonder instead
of worry,
the path forward changes.

Not because the world shifts.
But because you do.

You're no longer forcing yourself to become someone else.
You're starting to believe that who you already are—
right here, right now—
is someone worth returning to.

Key Takeaways

- Imagination is not just for creating outwardly—it can be used to care inwardly.

- Self-compassion begins with envisioning a gentler way to relate to yourself.

- Rewriting the inner voice isn't denial—it's healing.

- Imagination lets you see yourself as growing, not failing.

- Meeting yourself with softness is a deeply creative act—and a powerful act of trust.

Slow Spark Practice

Rewrite the Voice:

Take a few minutes today to notice your inner voice in a moment of struggle.
Write down one critical sentence you often think. Something like:

- "I'm so behind."
- "Why can't I get this right?"
- "Everyone else is better at this."

Now—pause.
Take a breath.

Rewrite that sentence as if it came from a friend who loves you.
Let it be true. Let it be kind. Try:

- "I'm carrying a lot and still moving. That's strength."
- "This is hard, and I'm doing my best."
- "It's okay not to have it all figured out yet."

Keep both versions.
Read them aloud.
Notice how they feel in your body.

That's the beginning of self-compassion:
not erasing the struggle, but staying with it gently.

Let imagination be the doorway back to yourself—
not as you "should be,"
but as you already are.
Worthy.
Growing.
Enough.

Chapter 16: When the Spark Begins to Return

It doesn't arrive with a flourish.
No music. No fanfare.
No lightning bolt to declare: *You're back.*

It begins quietly.
Almost invisibly.

You're making tea, and a sentence passes through your
mind—
uninvited, unannounced.
It doesn't belong to your task list.
It belongs to something older.
A story, maybe. A memory.
A flicker of thought that feels warm and strange and famil-
iar all at once.

You're walking to the shop, and you notice the way light
touches a crumbling wall.
The curve of a cloud you once might've called a ship.
No one asks you to notice.
But you do.
Not because it's useful.
Because it stirs something.

You hum a tune without realizing.
You scribble a phrase on the corner of a receipt.
You catch an idea so light it feels like wind—
and for once, you don't let it blow away.

That's how it returns.
Not with fire.
Not with certainty.
But with flickers.

Brief, delicate moments of remembering.

The part of you that once played, once wondered, once
made things for no reason at all—
it doesn't shout.
It knocks.

And if you're rushing, you'll miss it.
But if you pause—just for a breath—
you'll feel it:
that little lift in your chest.
That tiny, quiet *yes.*

It's easy to doubt it.
To think you're pretending.
To say you're too old, too late, too tired.

But imagination doesn't care about that.
It doesn't need you to be ready.
It needs you to be open.

Because the moment you leave the door even slightly ajar,
it steps through.
Carefully.
Cautiously.
Checking if it's still welcome.

And if you meet it with gentleness—not expectation—
it lingers.

You reach for your notebook, not to write something *important*, but just to write.
You let your thoughts wander while washing dishes.
You follow a thread not because you know where it goes, but because something in you wants to follow it.

You stop dismissing those small sparks just because they're small.
You let them sit beside you.
You let them stay.

This isn't about a masterpiece.
It's about *motion*.
About remembering what it feels like to make *anything at all*.
To feel your inner life stretch out again—
not for applause,
but for breath.

And over time, something shifts.

You begin to see the world differently.
Not always.
Not every moment.
But often enough that it matters.

Colours feel brighter.
Silences feel deeper.
The hours don't pass so fast.

Not because your life has changed—
but because *you* have.

Because you stopped running.
Because you started listening.
Because you made space—quietly, patiently—
for the spark to return.

And it does.

Not as a flash.
But as a friend.
One who never left—
just waited until you remembered how to look for it again.

Key Takeaways

The spark doesn't return in grand moments—it comes in quiet flickers of presence and noticing.

You don't need a plan or project to be creative. You only need to be willing to pause.

Doubt is part of the process. But trust builds through small, repeated gestures of openness.

Imagination reawakens when we stop demanding and start listening.

You're not behind. You're returning. And even that is enough.

Slow Spark Practice

Keep the Door Ajar:

Try this for one week:

Each day, take five minutes to sit without a task.
No phone. No goal. Just stillness.

Let your mind drift. If a thought, image, or phrase arises that feels faintly alive—write it down.
Even if it's strange. Even if it's unfinished.

At the end of the week, read your notes aloud.
Not to analyse.
But to *witness*.

To remember that your imagination is still here—
still offering—
still waiting to be welcomed home.

Chapter 17: The Imagination in Others

When the spark begins to return in you, it doesn't stay contained.
It ripples outward. Quietly.

You start noticing it—not just in yourself, but in others.
In glimmers. In pauses.
In the way someone's voice catches when they speak about a long-shelved dream.
In how a child tells a story that changes shape mid-sentence—because their mind is moving faster than the words they know.
In a friend who says, *"I've had this idea for years,"* and then trails off before they can finish, already doubting its worth.

You begin to see something essential:
Imagination doesn't live alone.
It lives *between* us.
It wants to be shared, witnessed, welcomed.

It flickers quietly inside people who may never call themselves "creative"—
and yet, you can feel it, just beneath the surface, trying to reach the air.

Especially in children.

Children arrive in the world already fluent in imagination.
They don't need to be taught to wonder.
A couch becomes a spaceship.
A stick becomes a wand.
Rules are invented and broken mid-game.
They trust what feels vivid and alive, long before they're

taught what's "correct."

And yet—often without meaning to—we begin to dim that light.
We hand them devices that entertain but rarely invite them inward.
We replace open questions with preloaded apps.
Even toys now come with instructions, characters, storylines already chosen.

A LEGO set isn't a pile of maybe anymore.
It's a miniature model, with steps and stickers and a clear picture on the box
of what it's *supposed* to become.

We don't do this to harm them.
We do it because we think we're helping.
But what we're often teaching—quietly, steadily—is this:
The world prefers precision over play.
It's better to get it right than to make it your own.
Imagination is fine—for a while.
But eventually, it's time to grow up.

Except... children don't stop imagining because they grow up.
They stop because they feel imagination has no place here.
That it must be hidden, like a soft toy or a fairy tale.

But hidden is not gone.

And that's where we come in.
Not to reverse the pattern overnight,
but to *interrupt it*.
To leave the door ajar.
To become the kind of person who doesn't shut the story down when it sounds strange—
but leans in and says:
"Tell me more."

To protect someone's spark, you don't need a curriculum.

You need *attention*.
You need restraint—the patience not to correct or tidy too soon.
You need the willingness to be surprised.

Sometimes the most generous thing you can do is let someone be weird in front of you without flinching.
To hold their half-formed idea without rushing it into something safer.
To be a quiet witness to a thought still becoming.

And it's not just children who need that.

Your friend who used to sing but hasn't in years.
Your partner who doodles on receipts but never calls it art.
Your colleague who hesitates before sharing that wild idea in a meeting.
Every one of them is carrying something—
some glowing thread they've been too shy, too tired, or too trained to follow.

You can be the one who notices.
Who believes in it before they do.
Who reflects it back to them as something worthy—
not because it's polished,
but because it's *alive*.

The more you honor imagination in yourself, the more easily you'll recognize it in others.
It will glow more visibly.
Speak more clearly.
And when it does, your role changes.

You become part of something larger than personal renewal.
You become a protector of wonder.
A keeper of softness in a world that too often asks for edges.

You become someone who helps imagination survive—

by seeing it, by listening for it,
by leaving room for it to breathe.

Because sometimes, what someone needs most isn't advice or structure or solutions.
Sometimes, they just need someone to believe
that the strange, beautiful thing inside them is *real*.

And that's a kind of magic all its own.

Key Takeaways

- Imagination is not only personal—it's relational. It grows stronger when it's witnessed and encouraged.

- Children don't lose their imagination—they learn to hide it. Listening without correcting can help protect it.

- Adults carry quiet sparks, too. A single act of curiosity can help someone return to a long-forgotten part of themselves.

- You don't need to be a teacher to make a difference. Just a kind, present witness.

- The more you notice imagination in others, the more it flourishes in you—and in the world.

Slow Spark Practice

The Quiet Witness:

A practice in seeing. In soft noticing. In choosing presence over fixing.
You don't need a special setting—just a moment with another person
where imagination begins to peek through.

Step One: Make Space to Notice

Spend a few minutes today truly *watching* someone close to you—
without needing to direct or explain.
Notice where they linger.
What lights them up, even briefly.

If it's a child, follow their story—even if it makes no sense.
Ask, *"And then what happened?"* without steering it.
Let the world they're building be enough.

If it's an adult, pay attention to the places where they almost create,
almost share something delicate, almost say what they've long held inside.
You don't need to dig. Just offer gentle invitations:

"That sounds interesting."

"Tell me more."

"I love how your mind works."

Step Two: Respond Without Rescuing

Don't try to fix or finish their thought.
Let what's raw be raw. Let it stay.
This is a practice in not rushing the moment into something digestible.
It's a way of saying: *"I'm listening—even when it's uncertain."*

Step Three: Reflect Later
At the end of the day, jot down one spark you saw in someone else.
Whose imagination did you witness today?
How did it show up?

What did it feel like to see without needing to shape?

You might even ask yourself:

Who in my life might be quietly waiting for permission to imagine again?

How might I help them remember they're allowed?

You don't need a result.
Just the willingness to see softly.
Because when imagination is met with gentleness,
it always finds a way back to the surface.

Even in someone else's eyes,
you'll begin to feel your own spark flicker a little brighter.

Chapter 18: Imagination as a Way of Living

By now, something has likely shifted.

It might be quiet. It might be fragile.
But it's there—a thread you've begun to follow.
A thread that doesn't just lead to creativity in the traditional sense,
but to something far more foundational:
a different way of being in the world.

Imagination, once reawakened, doesn't stay contained.
It seeps into everything.
It changes not only *what* you do, but *how* you notice, how you speak, how you feel.
It becomes less about moments of brilliance
and more about a daily posture—
something woven into the way you observe, question, and move through your life.

You begin to notice what you once passed by—
the grain of wood beneath your fingertips,

the flicker of emotion in a stranger's face,
the curl of steam rising from your morning cup.

What once seemed small now feels alive.

Conversations stretch a little longer.
Silences aren't rushed to be filled.
There's more permission for things to be incomplete.
More wonder in things that used to feel routine.

You begin to leave space—
not just on your calendar, but in your thoughts.
You become less addicted to certainty.
You don't need every question to be answered,
every idea to be useful,
every moment to be optimized.

You start asking softer, more spacious questions:
What else might be true here?
What haven't I noticed yet?
What would happen if I let this be enough?

This is imagination not as output, but as *orientation*.
A way of living that replaces performance with presence.
A quiet rebellion in a culture obsessed with outcomes and
appearances.

You might find yourself walking slower.
Laughing more easily.
Letting your mind wander without tugging it back into or-
der.

You might start creating tiny rituals that have no measura-
ble purpose
but bring you an unexpected grounding—
watering a plant,
lighting a candle before you write,
taking the long route home
just to pass a street you like the look of.

And slowly—without fanfare—the shape of your life shifts.
Not drastically.
Not in cinematic scenes.
But in ways that feel more honest.
More yours.

Because when imagination becomes a way of living,
you no longer need permission
to see beauty,
to seek meaning,
to express wonder.

You stop waiting for the perfect moment to begin something.
You stop apologizing for what brings you joy.
You stop outsourcing your sense of aliveness
to someone else's idea of success.

And that's when the deepest shift takes place.

You return—
not to who you used to be,
but to who you've *always* been beneath the noise.
The version of you that still believes in possibility.
That still wants to explore.
That still knows how to dream—
not for applause,
but for connection.

To live with imagination is not to escape reality.
It's to *deepen* it.
To move through the world with an open heart,
an alert mind,
and the quiet belief that something sacred
might still be hidden in the ordinary.

And when you live like that,
the spark doesn't need to be found anymore.

It lives with you.

It breathes with you.
It becomes the way you move through the world.

Key Takeaways

- Imagination is not just for creating things—it's a way of moving through life.
  It changes how you speak, feel, notice, and relate to the world around you.

- Living imaginatively means valuing presence over performance.
  You begin to see beauty in the overlooked and allow wonder to arise without needing a reason.

- This way of living is slow, spacious, and deeply human. It welcomes mystery. It invites softness. It reconnects you with your truest self.

- Imagination doesn't require grand gestures.
  It only asks for attention—tiny acts of noticing that shape the texture of your days.

- You stop waiting for life to feel meaningful—
  and begin participating in making it so.
  Not with pressure.
  But with openness.
  And trust.

-

Slow Spark Practice

A Day Lived Differently:

This practice is simple:
Today, move through the world as if imagination were already part of you—
not something you reach for,
but something you carry.

Morning
Before you check your phone or write your to-do list, sit quietly for three minutes.
Ask:
What might today look like if I moved through it with curiosity, not just efficiency?
Jot down a word, an image, or a question that feels alive.
Let that be your companion.

Midday
In the middle of something routine—
washing dishes, commuting, refreshing your inbox—pause.
Notice one thing you've never noticed before.
Ask: *What story might this hold?*
You don't need an answer. You just need to wonder.

Evening
Light a candle. Pour a drink.
Sit in stillness for five minutes.
Reflect on the shape of your day.
Where did imagination show up?
What surprised you?
What felt different?

Write down three words that describe what it felt like to move through your day with an imaginative lens.

You don't need to change everything.
You only need to choose—gently and consistently—
to live with more attention,
more softness,
and more awe.

And the more you do,
the more imagination becomes not just something you remember—

but something you *are*.

Chapter 19: The Return of the Spark

The spark never truly leaves.

It flickers, yes. It quiets. It waits in corners we forget to check.
But it doesn't vanish—not really.
Even on the days when the world felt grey and hollow.
Even during the seasons when everything was noise and numbness.
It remained.
Not as a flame, but as an ember. A possibility.
A quiet pulse.

And maybe that's the most humbling, most beautiful truth of all:
Imagination does not abandon you.
It waits for you to remember.

It waits in the stray daydream you brushed aside.
In the story you kept rewriting in your head but never dared to tell.
In the strange memory that keeps returning, asking to be noticed.

It hides in the questions that never quite stopped tugging at you.
The ones that arrive late at night or mid-commute, soft as breath:
Could I still create something?
What if I tried again?
What if I never stopped?

The spark doesn't return with a bang.
It returns like breath you forgot you were holding—
a familiar rhythm beneath the rush of your days.
It returns not as something new,
but as something that was always yours.

This book hasn't *given* you the spark.
It's only reminded you where to look.

Not in someone else's masterpiece.
Not in the perfect routine.
Not in waiting for permission.

But in the folds of your own quiet noticing.
In the way you lingered before closing the notebook.
In the way your eyes softened when you saw beauty again
—and didn't rush to name it.

You've begun to carry the spark
not as a burden,
not as a goal,
but as a companion.

Something you walk with now.
Something you protect.

It lives in your choices:

In the moment you pause in conversation to wonder, not assume.
In the way you keep something strange, because it made you feel something.
In the scribbled idea that doesn't "make sense yet," but still gets written down.
In the space you hold for someone else's fragile idea—
without rushing to fix it.

That's how the spark lives.
Through your stewardship.
Through your return.
Again and again.

Even when you're tired.
Even when nothing comes.
Even when it would be easier to turn back to the noise.

And yes, life will get loud again.

Deadlines will pile up. Screens will beckon. Doubt will whis-

per.
That's not failure. That's just the world doing what it does.

But now you know the way back.

You know how to soften instead of push.
You know that *noticing* is more powerful than striving.
You know that imagination is not a luxury or a reward—
it is part of your human inheritance.

It doesn't ask for greatness.
It doesn't need applause.
It only asks for presence.
For your willingness to keep the door open—
even just a crack.

And the more you do,
the more it becomes second nature.

Not something you force.
Something you carry
into every conversation,
every silence,
every ordinary day.

Because now, you've remembered:

You are not just someone who creates.
You are someone who *listens* for wonder.
Someone who knows how to begin again.
Someone who keeps the spark alive—
not just in yourself,
but in others.

And when you do that,
you don't just reclaim imagination.

You reclaim your way of living.

You return to yourself—

and to the world—
with eyes open,
hands ready,
heart awake.

Key Takeaways

- The spark of imagination never disappears—it waits for your return.
  Even in times of silence or doubt, it remains quietly present, hoping to be noticed.

- You don't need to force creativity. You only need to soften, listen, and stay open.
  Imagination returns through gentle repetition and honest attention—not through pressure.

- Imagination lives not just in what you make, but in how you live.
  It shapes your relationships, your presence, your noticing.

- You are the keeper of the spark.
  By honoring your own creativity, you become someone who protects it in others, too.

- The journey doesn't end—it continues with you.
  Imagination is no longer something to find. It's something you carry.

Slow Spark Practice

The Ongoing Return:

This is a quiet ritual—meant to be revisited whenever the spark feels faint.

1. Create Stillness

Find a moment—any time of day—where you can sit with no goal.
No phone. No task. Just space.

2. Ask Gently
Close your eyes and ask:
Where did I notice a flicker today?
It might be a word, an image, a gesture, a question.
Let it come, however small.

3. Acknowledge the Spark
Open your eyes.
Write it down—a sentence, a phrase, a symbol.
Not to do anything with it.
Just to say: *I saw you. You matter.*

Repeat this as often as needed.

This is the practice now:
Not chasing the spark—
but walking with it.
Trusting that wherever you are,
it's already close by.

And so are you.

Chapter 20: Life After the Test Isn't a Test

There's a moment a lot of us carry—tucked away, somewhere deep.

You might not have told anyone about it.
You might not have even thought of it in years.
But it's there.

It comes after the noise has settled.
The test is over. The exam paper handed in. The classroom emptied.
Maybe you walked home in silence that day.

Maybe you didn't know what to feel.

There was supposed to be something—some kind of arriv-
al.
Some inner click of clarity that told you: "You did it. You're
on your way."

But instead... there was just stillness.
A quiet you couldn't quite explain.
Not peace, exactly—just a pause.

Like you were waiting for someone to tell you what it all
meant.

The world told you those tests were important.
Not just for your grades, but for your future. Your worth.
Your chances.

And so, you did what we all learned to do:
You studied hard. Memorized the right things.
Tried to guess what would be on the paper.

And maybe you did well.
Maybe you didn't.

But no matter how you scored, here's something they never said clearly enough:

The test was never the whole story.

It was just a snapshot—one small moment, taken under
pressure,
in a setting that rarely made room for wandering thoughts
or slow ideas
or the kind of quiet brilliance that doesn't fit into tick-box-
es.

It didn't measure how deeply you care.
It didn't see how long you think about the things that matter.

It didn't hear the way you ask questions that don't have easy answers.

And yet, for so many of us, that result stuck.
It became part of how we saw ourselves.

We began to think of ourselves as good or bad, capable or not—
based on a system that never truly saw the shape of who we were becoming.

But life outside of school?
It doesn't hand out grades.
It doesn't ask for your test scores.

It asks if you'll show up anyway.
If you'll keep learning.
If you'll keep trying, even when the next step is blurry.

Real life isn't something you pass or fail.
It's something you practice.

It's a conversation you keep having with yourself—
day by day,
choice by choice.

There are no final marks here. Just moments of decision:

Will you keep going after disappointment?
Will you forgive yourself when things fall apart?
Will you try something new without knowing how it will turn out?

That's the kind of courage no exam could measure.

That's what makes you strong—
not your ability to get it all right,
but your willingness to begin again,
and again,
and again.

So if you're still holding on to shame from a test you didn't do well in,
you can set it down now.

It never had the power to define you—not really.

If a number made you feel small, remember this:

You are not a number.
You are not a grade.
You are a person. A story. A spark.

And you are still unfolding.

Imagination wasn't on the exam.
But it might just be the thing that matters most in the life you're building now.

Because while scores tell us what we knew in one moment, imagination shows us what we're still capable of becoming.

And that's the real beginning.

Key Takeaways

• The exam was never the whole story.
It measured what you could recall under pressure—but not your depth, your curiosity, or your imagination.

• You are allowed to grow outside the lines.
School may have offered rules and grades, but life offers space. You get to shape your path.

• Real life isn't scored—it's lived.
You don't need to be ready. You just need to begin, and be willing to keep going.

• Mistakes don't define you.
Every stumble, every misstep, every strange detour can become part of your strength—if you let it.

• Your imagination is still with you.
Even if it was never on the syllabus, it's your most powerful guide now. Trust it.

Slow Spark Practice

Reclaiming the Story:

Find a quiet space where you won't be interrupted.

Take a few minutes to recall your final year at school—your last test, your results, or a time when you felt defined by a number or a score. Let the memory surface without judgment.

Now, write a letter.
Not to your teacher.
Not to the system.
But to *yourself at that age.*

Use the voice you've grown into today to speak to the version of you who thought the score would define everything.

You might say something like:

• "You were doing your best, and that was enough."

• "This number can't see your imagination, your kindness, your dreams."

• "You are not behind—you're just beginning."

When you finish, read the letter out loud. Slowly. As if you really mean it.
Because you do.
And that version of you still lives inside you, waiting for a little grace.

Chapter 21: The Imagination Compass

No one hands you a map when school ends.

There's no folded diagram tucked into your bag, no blink-ing arrow pointing to your destination. You step out into the world with a few facts, a handful of borrowed ideas, maybe even a plan—but not much certainty. And what sur-prises many of us—what no one really prepares us for—is just how *normal* that is.

Most people are making it up as they go.

Even the adults you once thought had it all figured out. They were walking through the fog too—smiling at wed-dings while worrying about rent, offering career advice while secretly wondering if they'd chosen the wrong path themselves. Beneath their confident answers were quiet doubts. They weren't always sure either.

Because here's the thing: most of adulthood isn't clarity. It's learning how to move with courage even when clarity doesn't show up.

And that kind of courage?
It doesn't come from having the full picture.
It comes from listening to something quieter.
Something older.
Something we're all born with, but slowly learn to doubt.

It comes from your imagination.

Not the version with glitter pens and storybooks. The deeper one. The one that acts like a compass—not draw-ing a map, but nudging you gently forward. It doesn't say, "This is the way." It whispers, *"I don't know where this leads, but something in me wants to find out."*

That's what imagination does.
It doesn't just help you dream—it helps you navigate.

It's the voice that says *try this* when logic says *don't*. The quiet hunch that stirs when something unknown but meaningful is nearby. It's not reckless. It's personal. It's how you begin to build a life that actually fits *you*—not someone else's template or timeline.

See, maps are tidy. They tell you where others have been. They work best in places already explored.

But you're not retracing someone else's route.
You're charting your own.

And that's where a compass is different.

A compass responds to where you are now—and where you're meant to be going, even if you can't see it yet.

That's scarier.
But it's also more honest.

We've been sold the story that life has right answers. That if you tick the right boxes—school, job, partner, house, pension—you'll land somewhere called *success*. But real life doesn't work like a checklist. It's made of strange turns, near-misses, old dreams that come back wearing new clothes, and moments of clarity that arrive late and unannounced.

The people who truly thrive?
They're not the ones with perfect plans.
They're the ones who learn how to feel their way forward.

They give themselves permission to change shape. To shift course. To not know for a while.

And here's something most people don't say:
The first thing you follow might *not* be it.

You might chase a dream that doesn't turn into anything. Take a job that feels wrong. Start something, then stop.

That's not failure.
That's how you learn how your compass works.

Because every detour still teaches direction.
Every "wrong turn" recalibrates the needle.

And every time something lights up inside you—even for a moment—that's not a mistake. That's the path whispering, *this way*.

A friend of mine once told me about a woman she knew—brilliant, successful, a corporate lawyer. But she felt like a stranger in her own life. One summer, she volunteered for a week in a community garden. It didn't make sense on paper. But the stillness, the earth beneath her fingernails, the slow rhythm of tending something alive—it brought her back to herself.

She didn't become a full-time gardener.
But that one quiet week changed everything.

She went on to design green spaces in city offices—places for tired minds to breathe again. She built something no one else thought to build.
Because her compass pointed somewhere new.

That's the beauty of imagination.

It doesn't shout. It tugs. It stirs. It nudges you toward what feels alive—even when you can't explain why.

So how do you know which direction to follow?

Start by asking:

What do I keep thinking about when no one's asking anything of me?

What feels oddly alive, even if I don't know why?

What keeps returning like a quiet question I haven't answered yet?

You won't always know what it means.
But that's okay.

Compasses don't need certainty. They just need motion.
The more you walk, the more they adjust.

And the more honest you are with yourself, the clearer the needle becomes.

Take the next step.
Even if it's odd.
Even if it surprises people.
Even if it surprises *you*.

Because this life?

It's not a test.
It's not a race.
It's not a performance.

It's yours to explore.

And your imagination?

It's ready to lead.

Key Takeaways

The Imagination Compass

- **You don't need a map—you need a compass.**
  Life isn't linear. Your path unfolds as you walk it, and your imagination helps you find your way.

- **Everyone's figuring it out.**
  Even the most confident people are walking through fog. You're not behind.

- **Imagination guides when logic can't.**
  It doesn't guarantee answers—but it gives you direction.

- **Detours aren't failures—they're information.**
  Every turn helps you know yourself better. Nothing is wasted.

- **That quiet pull is worth listening to.**
  Even if others don't get it. Even if it doesn't "make sense" yet. If it stirs you—it matters.

Slow Spark Practice

Listening to Your Compass:

Find a quiet space without distractions.

Close your eyes. Take three slow breaths.

Then gently ask yourself:

"What am I quietly curious about right now?"

Don't rush the answer. Let your mind wander.

Now write this sentence three times, each with a different ending:

"Lately, I've been feeling drawn to..."

Let the answers be small, strange, or surprising.

Maybe it's a book topic, a hobby you used to love, a place you dream about, or a type of conversation that makes you feel more *you*.

Now underline the one that feels like it holds a little *weight*—or makes your chest feel a little lighter.

You don't need to act on it today.
Just notice it. Name it.

That's your compass whispering.

And even noticing it?

That's a step.

Chapter 22: Fuel for the Long Road

There's a story many of us were given early on—and most of us never thought to question it.

The idea that education ends. That one day, after enough essays and exams and well-behaved participation, we'll arrive. We'll graduate. The world will open its arms. We'll have a plan—and the confidence to carry it out.

But here's what that story forgets to mention:

Life doesn't begin at the finish line of a test.

It begins the moment no one is grading you anymore.
The moment the checklist disappears.
And you're left with a different set of questions.

Not *"Did I pass?"*
But *"What now?"*
"Who am I becoming?"
"What do I do when nothing goes to plan?"

These aren't multiple-choice.
They don't come with rubrics or model answers.
But they shape your life far more than anything that ever

appeared on a final exam.

And when the old routes vanish—when the map goes quiet, when the certainty dissolves—what gets you through isn't how well you memorized the past.

It's how gently, how bravely, you can imagine what comes next.

Because imagination isn't just the spark of a good idea. It's not limited to the canvas or the stage or the sketchbook.

It's the quiet fuel that keeps you moving when the road gets long.

It whispers, *There's still something here to notice,*
even when you feel tired.
It nudges, *Try this,*
even when everything seems stuck.

We tend to treat imagination like a luxury.
A bonus if there's time.

But out here—in the shifting, beautiful, unpredictable terrain of real life?

It's not extra.
It's essential.

You'll face seasons of uncertainty. Days that feel flat. Moments when the path you'd been walking suddenly disappears beneath your feet. You'll watch others race ahead while you're quietly wondering if you've taken a wrong turn.

In those moments, logic might sit quietly in the backseat. Plans might dissolve in your hands.

But imagination—the kind that listens, adjusts, dreams

quietly—will still be there beside you.

Not to rescue you with the perfect answer.
But to remind you:

You still have tools.
You are not finished.
Something new is always possible.

That's why it matters to keep your imagination alive—not just in the moments that feel creative, but especially in the ones that don't.

In the dull hours.
In the slow chapters.
In the long, uncertain stretches.

Because the road you're on isn't straight. It loops. It stutters. It changes without warning.

And while that can feel exhausting, it also means this:

You're free to choose again.

To change direction.
To ask different questions.
To grow in a way no one else saw coming.

Every step becomes part of the learning.
Every breakdown, every strange detour, every awkward first attempt teaches you something—about resilience, about attention, about what matters to you now.

You'll learn not just from what succeeds, but from what falls apart.

And slowly, you'll begin to notice:
It's not speed that sustains you.
It's softness.
Curiosity.

The small, steady decision to keep going—even when you're unsure.

You don't need to see the whole path to take the next step.
You don't need certainty to move.
You only need to remain open.

That's where the spark lives now.
Not in the textbook.
Not in the perfect five-year plan.

But in your courage to try again—with gentleness, with honesty, and with hope.

Because what fuels the long road isn't brilliance.
It isn't certainty.
It's the quiet decision to remain *willing*—to believe that even here, something new can begin.

And if you can keep choosing that?

You'll go further than you can imagine right now.

Key Takeaways

Fuel for the Long Road

- **Learning doesn't end when school does.**
  It deepens through experience, reinvention, and attention to what's unfolding.

- **Imagination isn't something you outgrow.**
  It's something you grow *into*—again and again.

- **Real life won't hand you a syllabus.**
  But it will offer you moments—strange, beautiful, difficult ones—that call for presence and courage.

- **Thriving doesn't come from certainty.**
  It often comes from curiosity, and from being willing to

keep learning as you go.

- **Imagination is your endurance.**
  Not because it fixes everything—but because it keeps you *moving* through everything.

Slow Spark Practice

Refuelling Yourself:

This week, choose a quiet moment.
After a walk. Before bed.
Somewhere you can sit still, without rushing.

Then ask yourself gently:

What am I carrying that feels heavy right now?

What have I been quietly wondering about lately?

If I didn't have to get it "right," what would I try next?

Write down whatever comes. No judgment. No filter.

Then circle one word or phrase that feels *alive*.
Let it sit with you. Let it simmer.

That flicker you feel?

That's the spark.

Even if it's quiet—it's still there.
And that's enough to begin.

Chapter 23: Five Sparks That Outlived the System

True stories of people who "failed" the test—but passed the one that mattered most.

Before you tell yourself you're too far behind... before you let a grade, a rejection, or a forgotten report card define you... read these.

These aren't superheroes. These are people who didn't fit the mould.
People who were told: You're not smart enough. You're too slow. You're not ready.
People who walked away from the system—but not from themselves.

What they had wasn't permission.
It wasn't a plan.

It was a spark.
An inner pull. A stubborn kind of imagination that kept whispering, There's more.

This is your reminder:
School ends. Learning doesn't.
And life will always have room for the ones who dare to imagine a different way forward.

Real Lives, Real Sparks: Stories That Prove the Test Isn't Everything

1. The Dropout Who Built an Empire

Richard Branson – *Left school at 16*

"You don't learn to walk by following rules. You learn by doing, and by falling over."

Richard Branson struggled deeply with dyslexia. Traditional schooling felt impossible. Teachers mistook his learning difference for laziness or lack of intelligence. By age 16, he'd dropped out completely.

But that wasn't the end. It was the beginning.

Branson started a magazine called *Student*, then a mail-order record company. That tiny venture became Virgin Records, which eventually grew into the Virgin Group—spanning airlines, music, media, fitness, even space travel.

He became one of the most influential entrepreneurs of our time—not because he followed the rules, but because he refused to be defined by them. He used imagination as a business tool, building a life of wild ideas, risk-taking, failure, and reinvention.

Branson never finished school. But he learned to trust the spark school couldn't measure.

Food for the Soul:

Sometimes the world says you're not ready. That doesn't mean you're not capable. It means your journey is meant to begin elsewhere—on your own terms, with your own spark.

2. The Poet With No Diploma

Maya Angelou – No formal college education

"You can't use up creativity. The more you use, the more you have."

Maya Angelou didn't follow the expected path. No college degree. No polished résumé. Her early life was marked by trauma, silence, and displacement. For years, she stopped speaking altogether.

But her silence wasn't emptiness—it was observation. And when she finally found her voice, she had something to say. The world listened.

She became a poet, singer, dancer, actor, activist, and teacher. Her memoir, *I Know Why the Caged Bird Sings*, became a literary landmark. She received more than 50 honorary doctorates and read at a U.S. presidential inauguration.

She didn't need a diploma. She used life as her teacher—and imagination as the way back to herself.

Food for the Soul:

Even in your quietest, most uncertain moments, your imagination is still listening. And when you're ready, it will help you speak—not just for yourself, but for those still searching for their voice.

3. The "Unteachable" Genius

Thomas Edison – Expelled from school for being "addled"

"I have not failed. I've just found 10,000 ways that won't work."

Thomas Edison lasted just three months in school. His teacher called him "addled"—an old word for slow or confused. His mother disagreed. She pulled him out and taught him herself.

That belief changed everything.

Edison didn't learn from textbooks. He learned by experimenting. By failing. By trying again. He filled notebooks with ideas—and turned more than 1,000 of them into patents.

He invented the lightbulb, the phonograph, and the motion picture camera. He helped shape modern life.

But the system didn't see his brilliance. It couldn't.
He succeeded not because he fit the model, but because he trusted his own way of thinking—even when others didn't.

Food for the Soul:

When the world labels you as too slow, too different, or too much—don't shrink to fit. Let your imagination be the teacher that school never was.

4. The Storyteller Who Struggled to Read

Whoopi Goldberg – Dropped out, dyslexia

"We're here for a reason. I believe a bit of the reason is to throw little torches out to lead people through the dark."

Whoopi Goldberg couldn't read fluently for years. School made her feel broken. Teachers didn't understand dyslexia, and she was led to believe she was dumb. Eventually, she dropped out.

But she wasn't broken. She was becoming something else.

She worked odd jobs—bricklayer, mortuary cosmetologist—while performing in small theaters. Her one-woman stage show caught Steven Spielberg's attention, leading to her breakout role in *The Color Purple*.

She went on to win an Emmy, Grammy, Oscar, and Tony—one of the few artists ever to do so.

Whoopi didn't need the system to recognize her.
She needed space to be fully, wildly herself.

Food for the Soul:

You don't have to learn like everyone else to shine. Sometimes, the very thing that made you feel slow in school is the same thing that makes you powerful in the world.

5. The Apple That Fell Far From the Tree

Steve Jobs – Dropped out of college after 6 months

"Have the courage to follow your heart and intuition. They somehow already know what you truly want to become."

Steve Jobs left college after six months. He slept on friends' floors and attended only the classes that intrigued him—like calligraphy. Years later, that "useless" class would inspire the elegant design of the Macintosh.

Jobs co-founded Apple in a garage at age 21. He didn't chase success. He followed fascination. And even when he was forced out of the company he built, he didn't quit—he started again.

Pixar. NeXT. Then back to Apple. Then the iPhone.

His path wasn't predictable. It wasn't tidy.
But it was imaginative. And it changed everything.

Food for the Soul:

Sometimes the thing that doesn't make sense to anyone else is the exact thing you're meant to pursue. Trust the path that lights you up—even if no one else can see where it leads.

The spark isn't about having the answers.

It's about asking better questions.

It's not about getting it right.
It's about staying alive to what lights you up.

These people didn't pass every test.
But they passed the one that mattered most:

They never stopped imagining what life could be.

Epilogue: Light Carried Forward

If you've made it here, something has already shifted.
Not everything. Not all at once. But something.
A thread has been pulled loose. A little more space has
opened inside your mind.

The world feels different—not because it has changed, but
because you're looking with different eyes.

That's what the spark does.
It doesn't shout.
It glows.

And now that you've seen it—truly seen it—it's harder to
ignore.

This wasn't a manual.
It wasn't a formula.
It wasn't a set of steps to follow.

It was a walk back to something you never truly lost.

You don't need to remember every word.
You don't need to hold on to every idea.

What matters is what you carry forward:
The softness.
The wonder.
The slow permission to be fully alive again.

And if you forget—because you will, we all do—know this:

You can return.

You can return to your imagination like a garden—neglected, maybe, but never ruined.
Ready to be tended.
Ready to grow.

You can return to the small rituals that remind you who you are.
To the stories, the sketches, the thoughts you didn't chase before.
To the version of yourself that still knows how to feel wonder.

No matter how far you wander.
No matter how long it's been.

The spark waits without judgment.

It doesn't need you to be perfect.
It only asks that you come back with your whole self—and stay long enough to listen.

So take this spark and carry it.
Into your conversations.
Into your work.
Into your parenting, your friendships, your art.

Into the quiet moments when no one is watching.

Let it guide how you see.
How you imagine.
How you live.

And when you pass someone who seems like they've forgotten their own spark—
light a small one for them, too.

Not loudly.
Not dramatically.
Just enough to help them remember:

They still carry it.
And always have.

Printed in Dunstable, United Kingdom